FILTER OF TRUTHYNESS AND FACTS

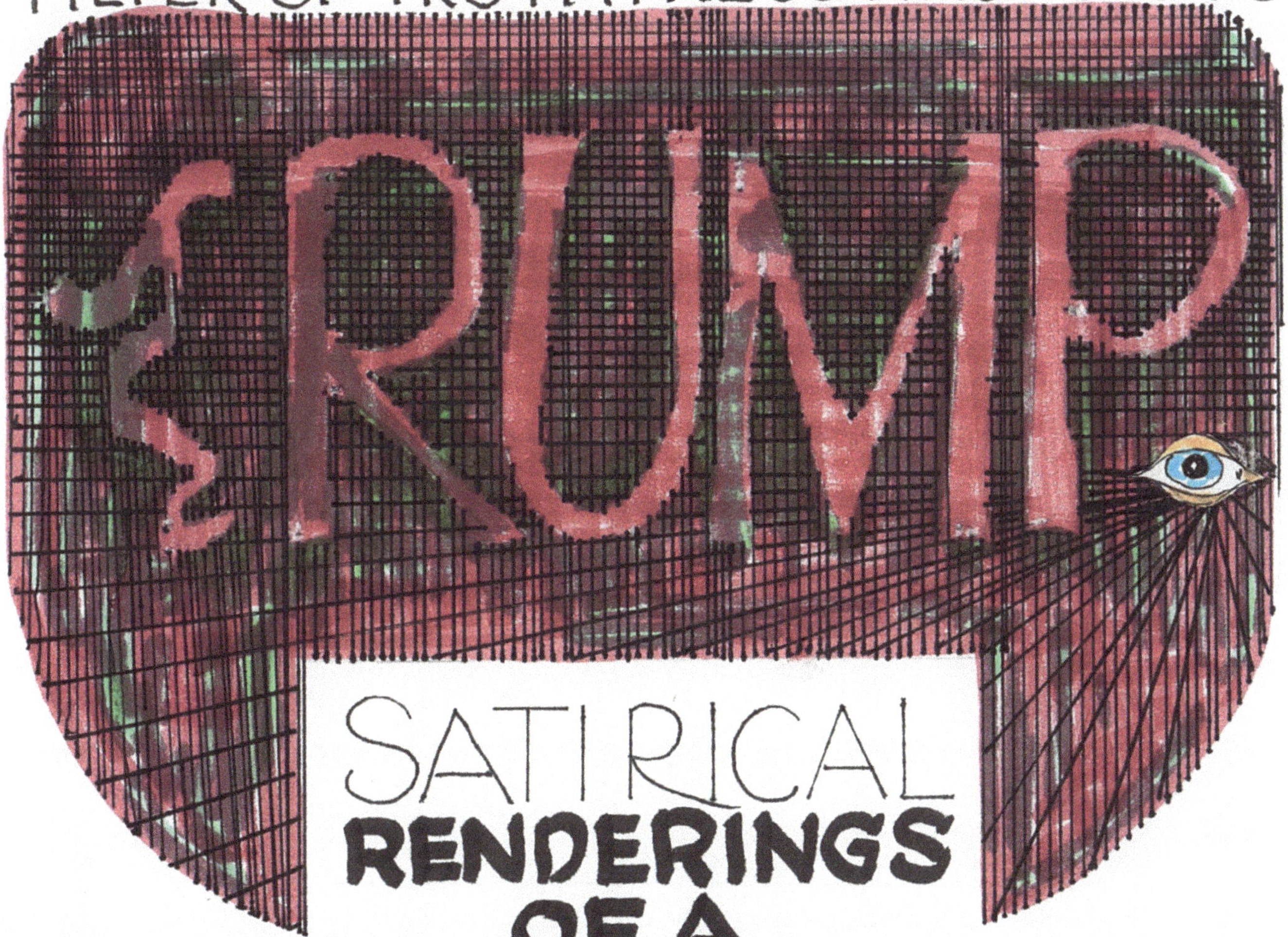
TRUMP

SATIRICAL RENDERINGS OF A DESPICABLE THINGY NAMED DONALD J. TRUMP

Lost Coast Press
Fort Bragg ,California

Copyright © 2023 by Donald Willis

For more information and to buy additional copies,
please contact Lost Coast Press:
155 Cypress Street, Suite A
Fort Bragg CA 95437
cypresshouse.com
800-773-7782

ISBN: 978-1-935448-47-1

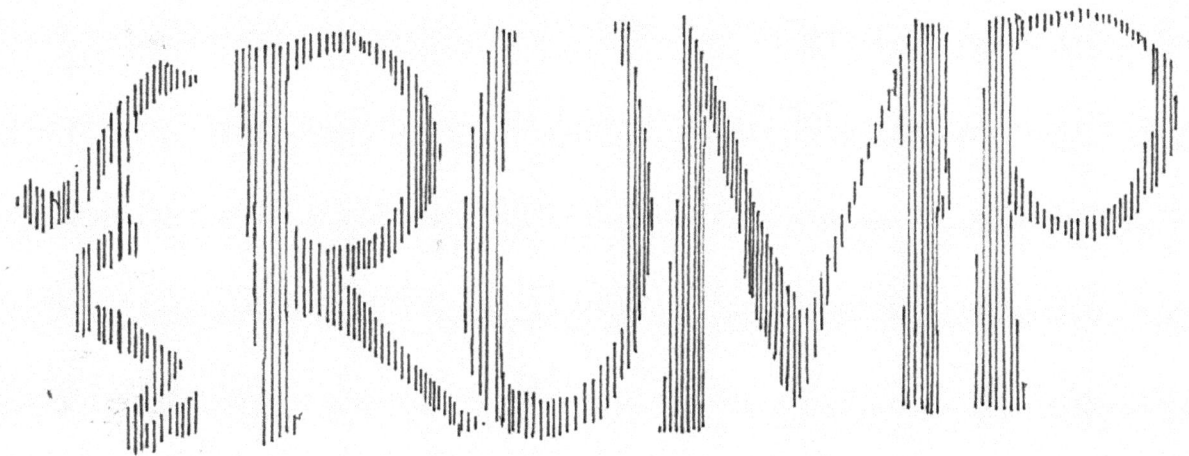

INTRODUCTION

This is a short story of a tragedy unwinding over four years. A story told by satirical illustration and text. This story shows how a pathological person who takes what he wants, gets in power to be president, stays in power after two impeachments and damn near remains a president after causing a riot at the White House. This story is by Don Willis with some exaggeration, but generally truthful.

Why?

Why was Trump exempt from the rules for reporting his income-taxes before he became president? That one rule would have stopped him from being president. Why was that one rule broken? Who's in charge of all the rules? ? ? ? All former presidents had to show their income-tax forms.

Why does all problems end up in litigation when the rules have been already established? Who knows? The shadow knows...

2016

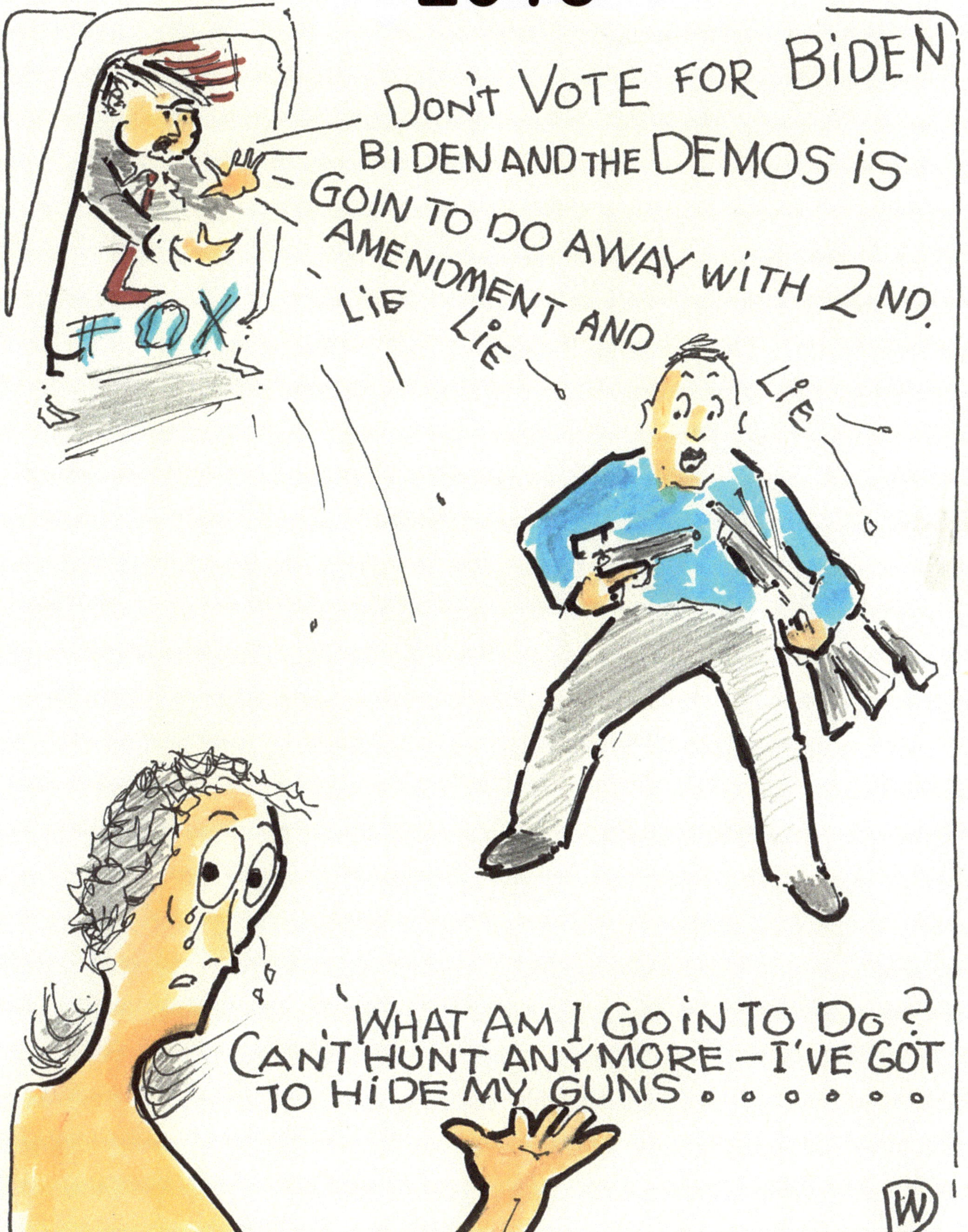
DON'T VOTE FOR BIDEN
BIDEN AND THE DEMOS IS GOIN TO DO AWAY WITH 2ND. AMENDMENT AND
FOX
LIE LIE LIE
WHAT AM I GOIN TO DO? CAN'T HUNT ANYMORE - I'VE GOT TO HIDE MY GUNS.......
W.

TRUMP

"Don't say that name" It makes me ill. If you say that name again just leave the first letter off . . . and pronounce the last four letters. What does it spell ??? - **RUMP.** Exactly. That suits him fine.

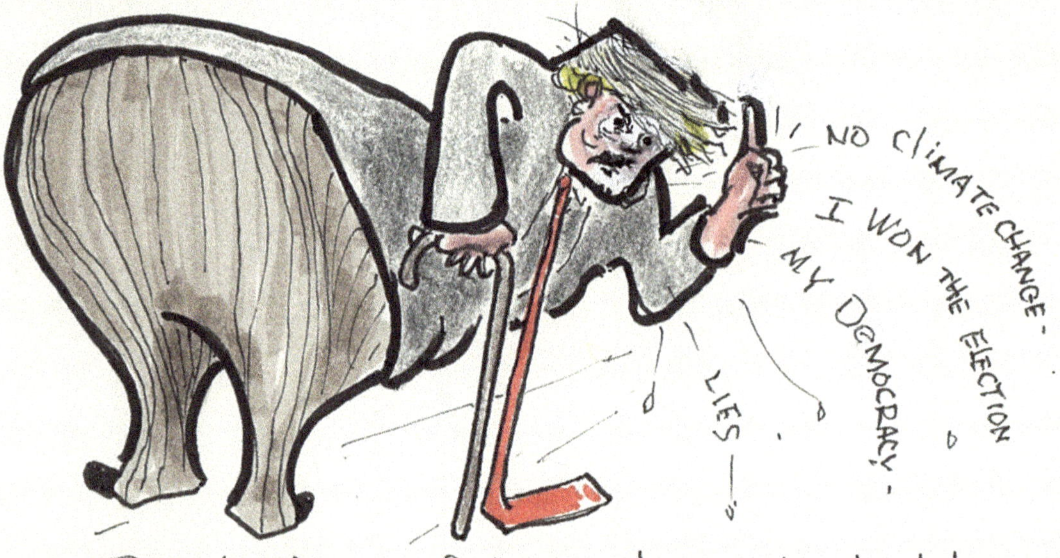

NO CLIMATE CHANGE -
I WON THE ELECTION
MY DEMOCRACY -
LIES

Break free of his strangle hold on democracy . . Get vaccinated, think green, love thy neigbor and vote for someone who has love for all living things and knows the difference between right and wrong in the moral and spiritual sense. NO MORE LIES.

What Power in A Single Lie?

Why is morality on certain subjects different in meaning and importance within a society? A great president can be impeached for a personal sex act that was discovered and then blasted to the media, while that same high office of our country can be completely engaged in lies and exaggerations and bent on changing our whole democracy without consequence.

Here's a question to think about and maybe change some rules before the great election in 2020. What if it was a felony to lie about your opponent in a speech and that lie was meant to demean and lower the opinion of the audience and viewers of television? Do you think it fair to do so? Would you like someone to relate untrue things about you? Do you think that someone who is looked upon with great admiration who is telling a lie would be believed? You betcha! Most everyone in earshot would believe. Do you think that the person who's being lied about has a way of defending themselves after the lie was spoken? Almost everyone would believe that lie, no matter how much they protested.

Who do we know in the present political circus that speaks about people and everything with exaggeration and has lied every day for the past two years and nine months on news media? I believe a single lie should be a felony in that context and the prevaricator, after a short court trial, be sent swiftly to prison for five years of hard labor or worse. Our whole belief system is being swallowed up by lies and we orally have to stop and ponder the truth. Let's make that single lie a felony.

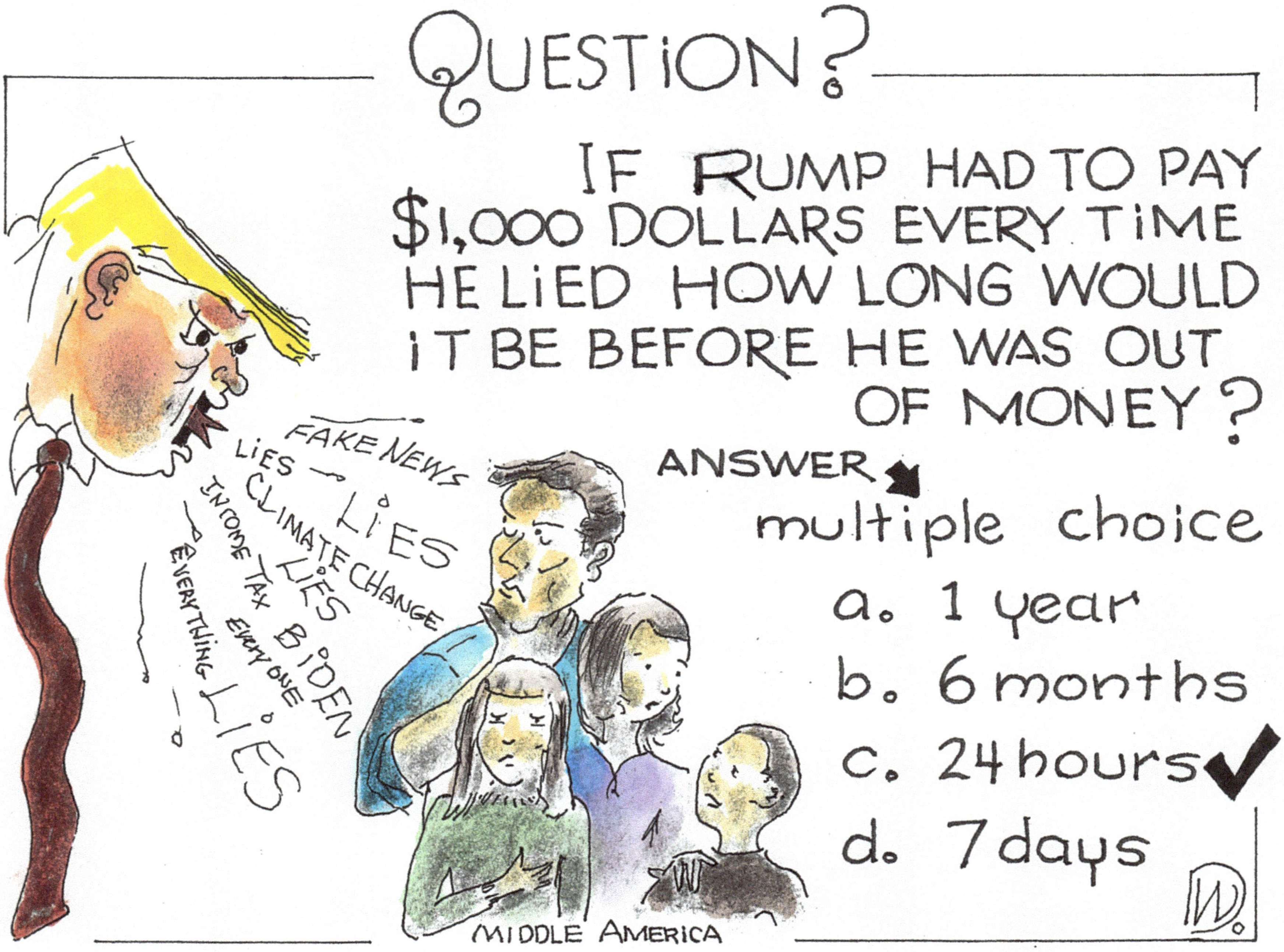
QUESTION?
IF RUMP HAD TO PAY $1,000 DOLLARS EVERY TIME HE LIED HOW LONG WOULD IT BE BEFORE HE WAS OUT OF MONEY?
ANSWER
multiple choice
a. 1 year
b. 6 months
c. 24 hours
d. 7 days
FAKE NEWS
LIES
LIES
CLIMATE CHANGE
LIES
INCOME TAX
BIDEN
EVERY ONE
EVERYTHING
LIES
MIDDLE AMERICA

2020

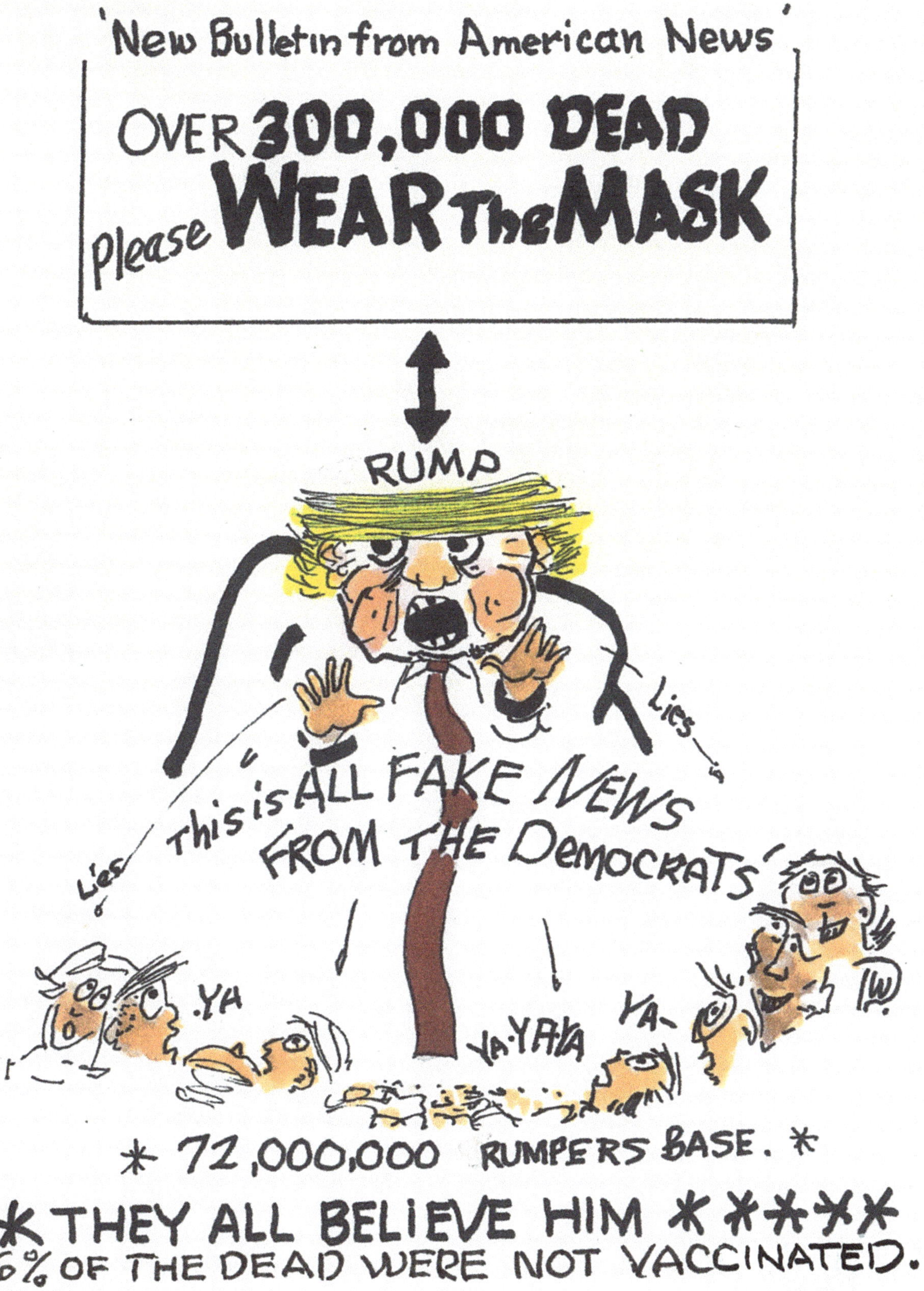
'New Bulletin from American News'
OVER 300,000 DEAD
please WEAR The MASK
RUMP
Lies
'this is ALL FAKE NEWS FROM THE DEMOCRATS'
Lies
YA
YA-YA YA
YA-
* 72,000,000 RUMPERS BASE. *
* THEY ALL BELIEVE HIM *****
86% OF THE DEAD WERE NOT VACCINATED.

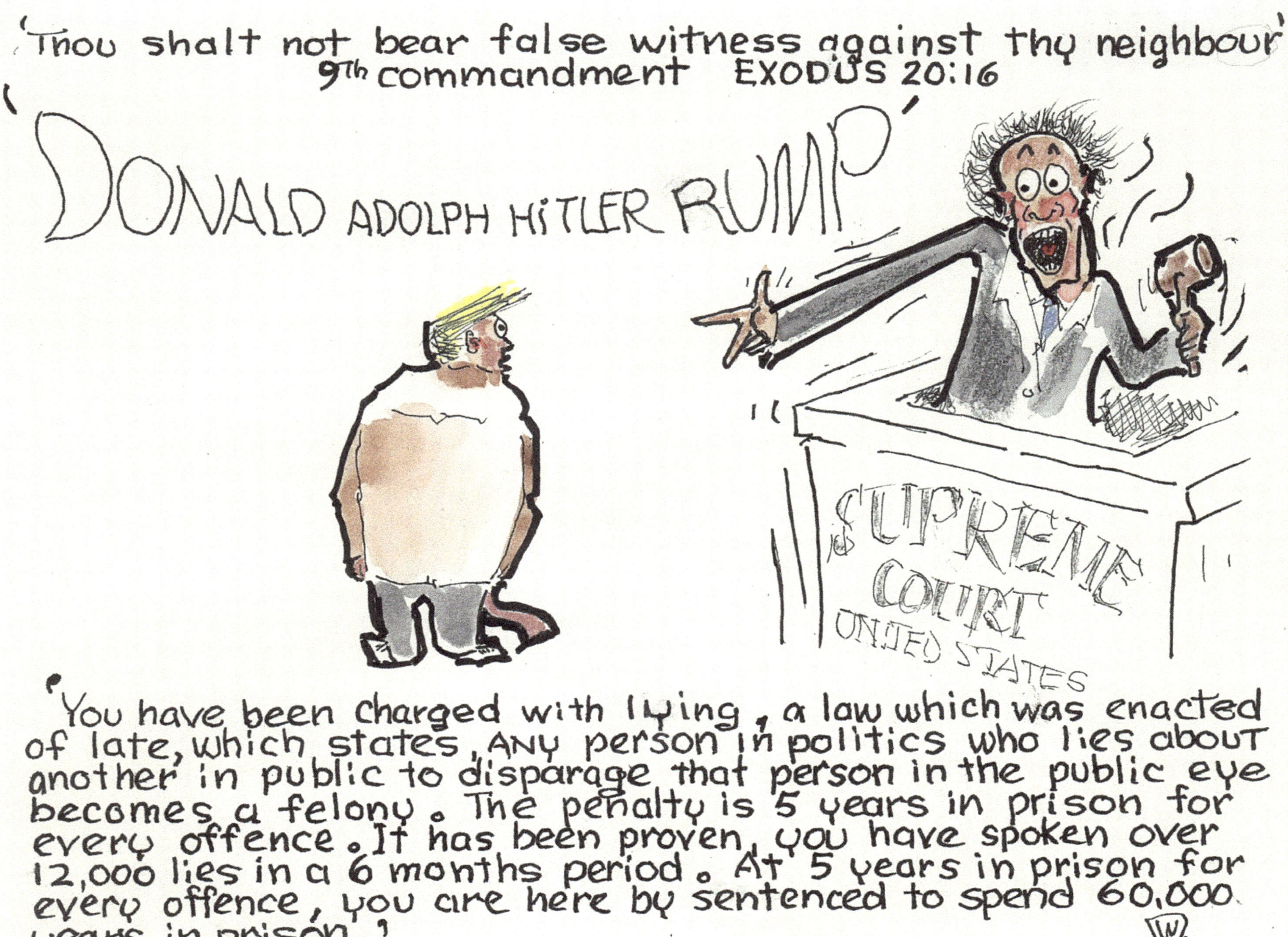

'Thou shalt not bear false witness against thy neighbour'
9th commandment EXODUS 20:16
'DONALD ADOLPH HITLER RUMP'
SUPREME COURT UNITED STATES
'You have been charged with lying, a law which was enacted of late, which states, ANY person in politics who lies about another in public to disparage that person in the public eye becomes a felony. The penalty is 5 years in prison for every offence. It has been proven, you have spoken over 12,000 lies in a 6 months period. At 5 years in prison for every offence, you are here by sentenced to spend 60,000 years in prison.'
W.

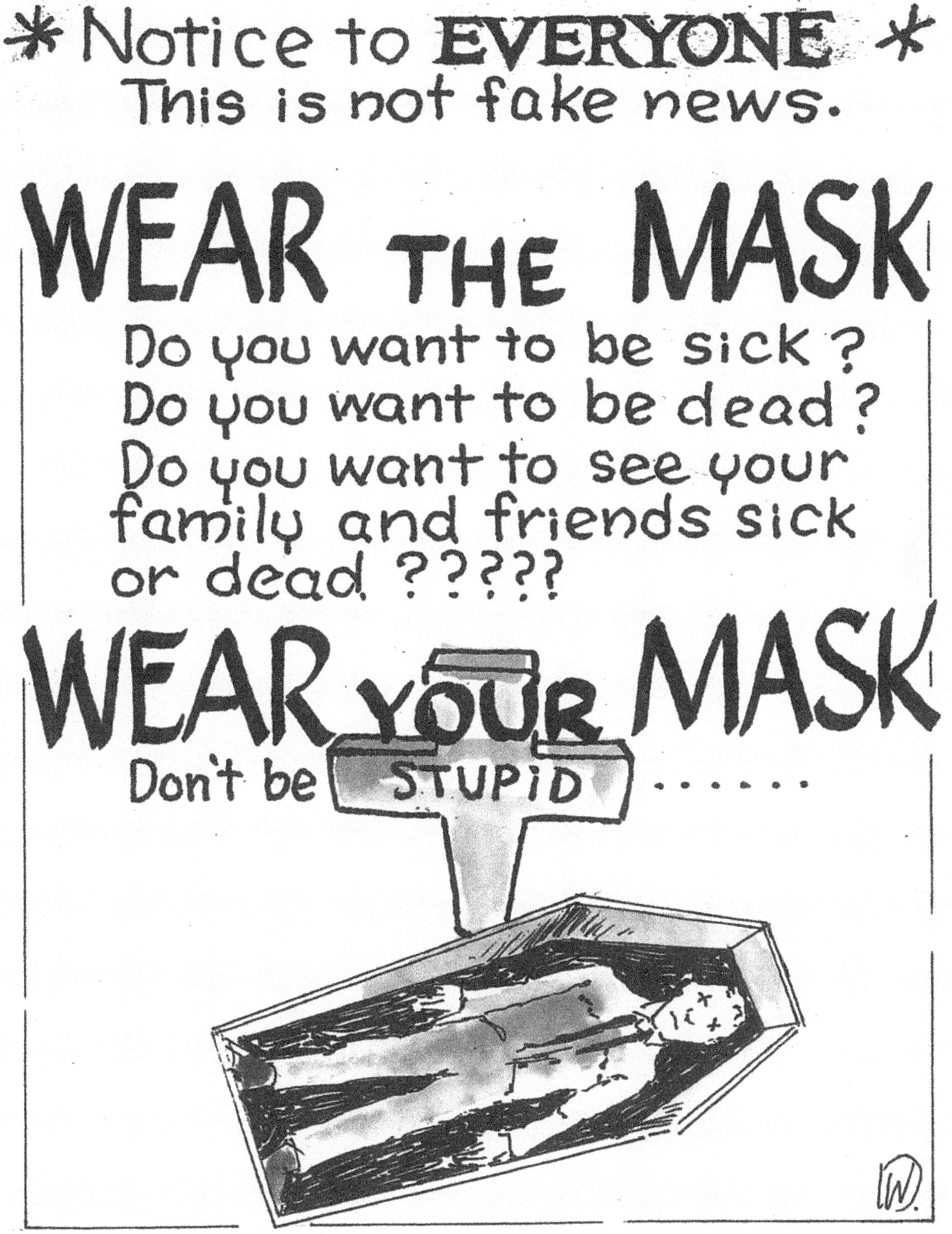
* Notice to EVERYONE *
This is not fake news.
WEAR THE MASK
Do you want to be sick?
Do you want to be dead?
Do you want to see your family and friends sick or dead?????
WEAR YOUR MASK
Don't be STUPID ......
W.

BIDEN WON
SHUT UP
WEAR A MASK
GET OVER IT

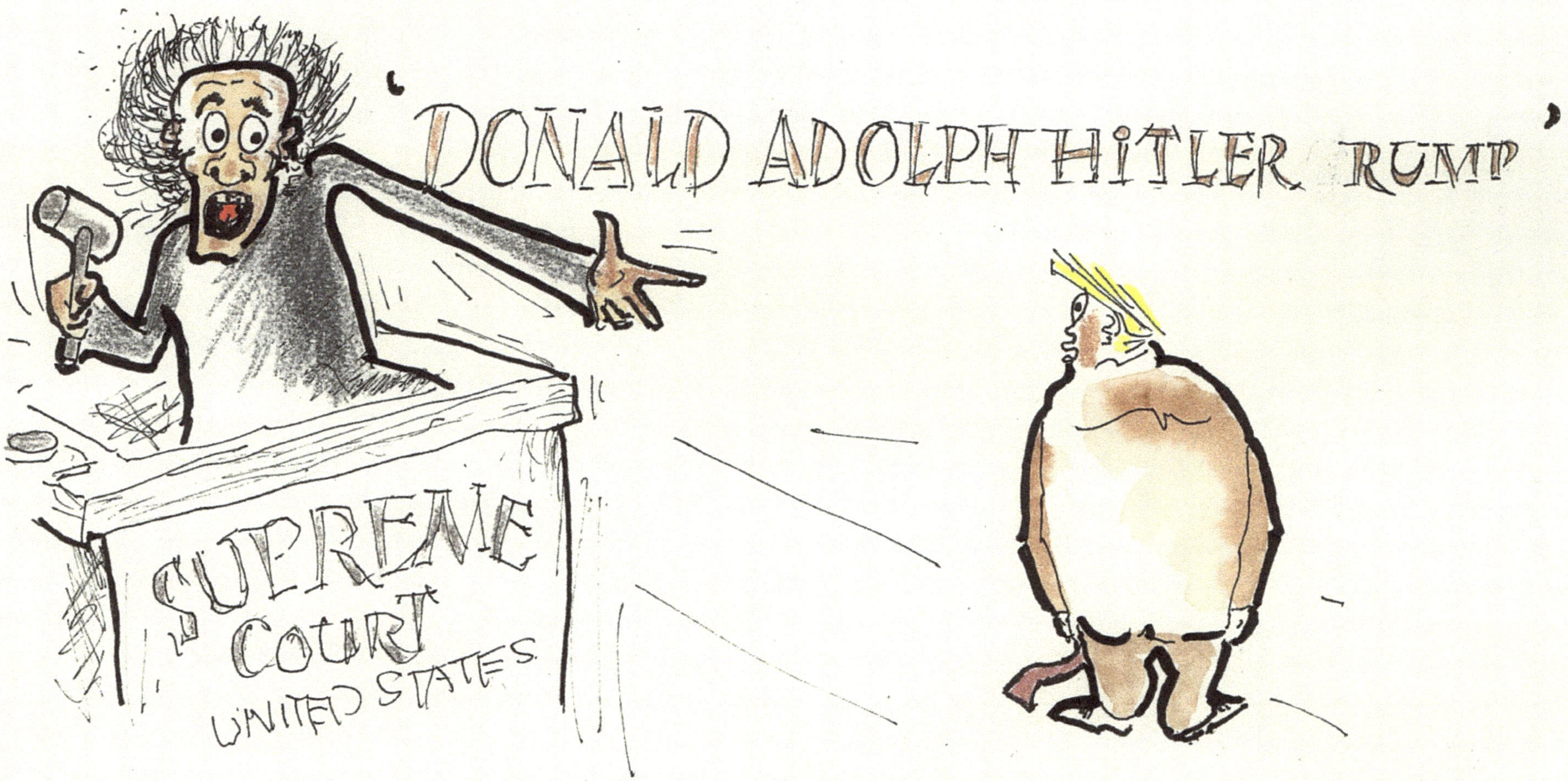
'DONALD ADOLPH HITLER RUMP'
SUPREME COURT
UNITED STATES

'YOU HAVE BEEN CHARGED WITH THE MURDER OF ~~233,000~~ 255000 PEOPLE OF THE UNITED STATES BECAUSE YOU DID NOTHING AT ALL TO HELP THE PEOPLE. THE PENALTY IS 50 YEARS IN PRISON FOR EVERY PERSON WHO DIED IN THE COVID-19 PANDEMIC. YOU ARE SENTENCED TO 11,650,000 YEARS IN PRISON OR UNTIL YOUR DEAD.'

WJ.

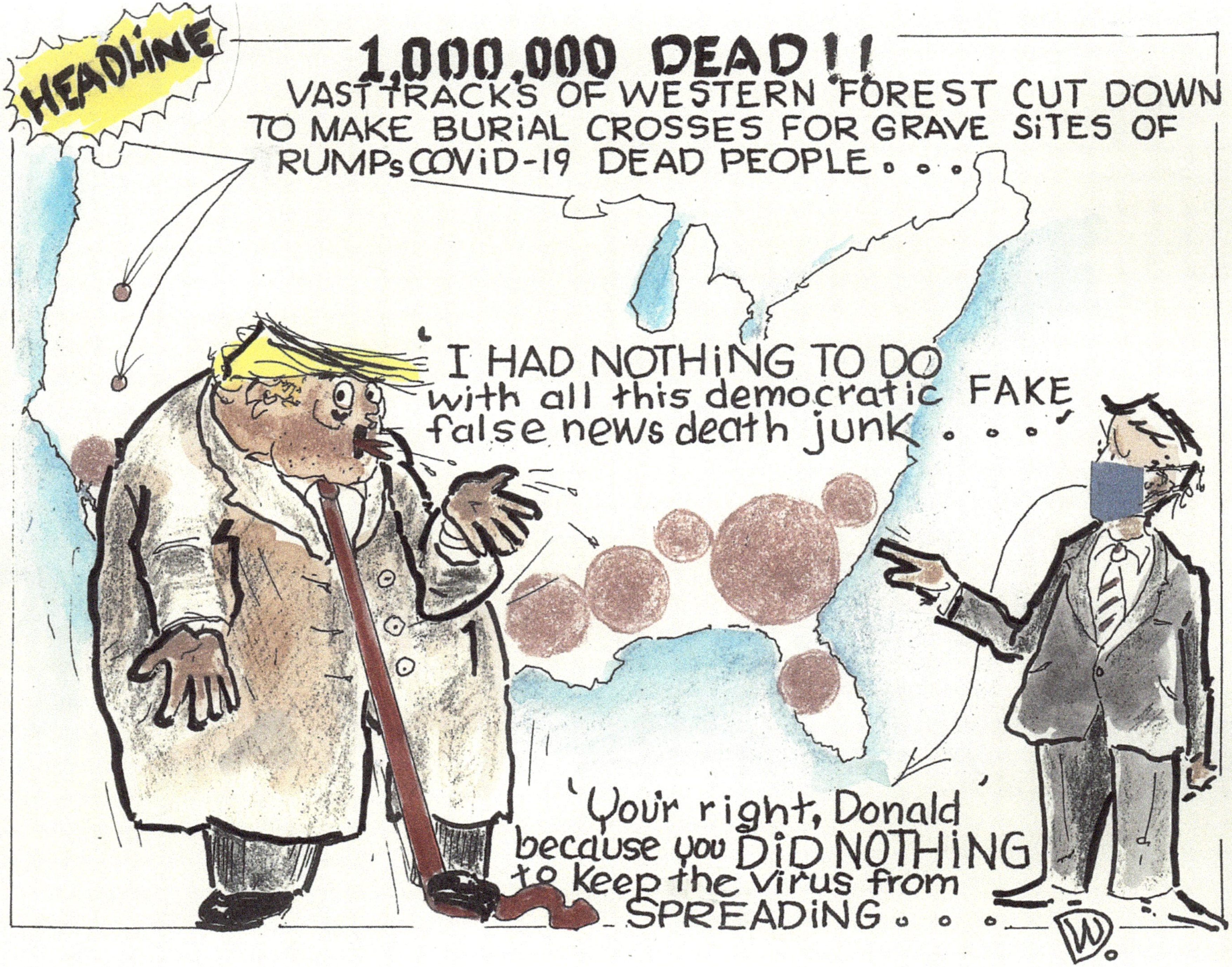
HEADLINE
1,000,000 DEAD!!
VAST TRACKS OF WESTERN FOREST CUT DOWN TO MAKE BURIAL CROSSES FOR GRAVE SITES OF RUMPs COVID-19 DEAD PEOPLE...
'I HAD NOTHING TO DO with all this democratic FAKE false news death junk...'
'Your right, Donald because you DID NOTHING to keep the virus from SPREADING...'
W

Would the covid pandemic still be with us today if Rump had insisted people to wear a mask when he was in office?

DO YOU REALLY WANT TO GO IN FOR YOUR COVID-19 SHOT?

1st. SHOT
EARLY 2ND SHOT

DIRECT ORDER FROM WASHINGTON BEFORE ELECTION, 2020.

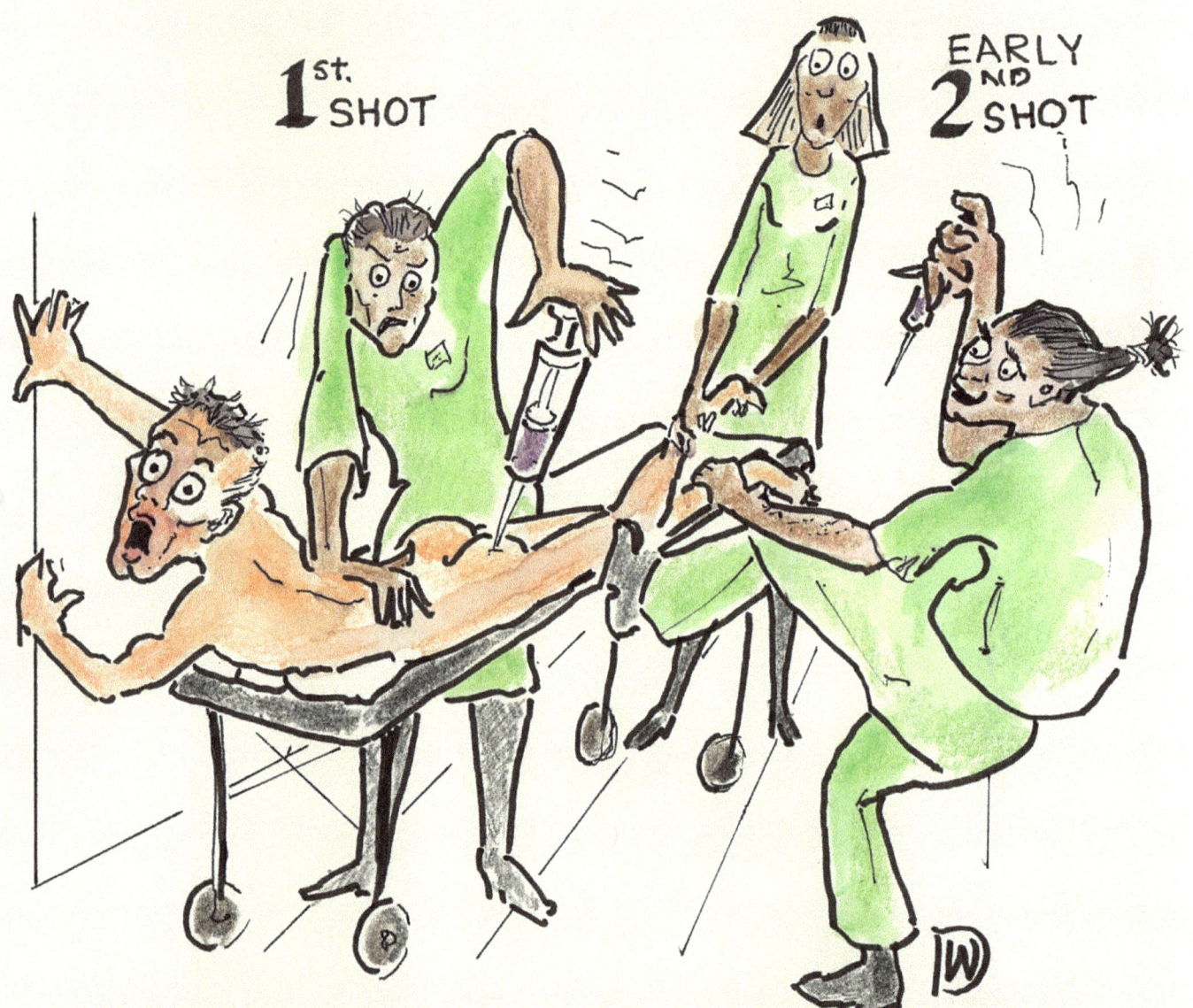

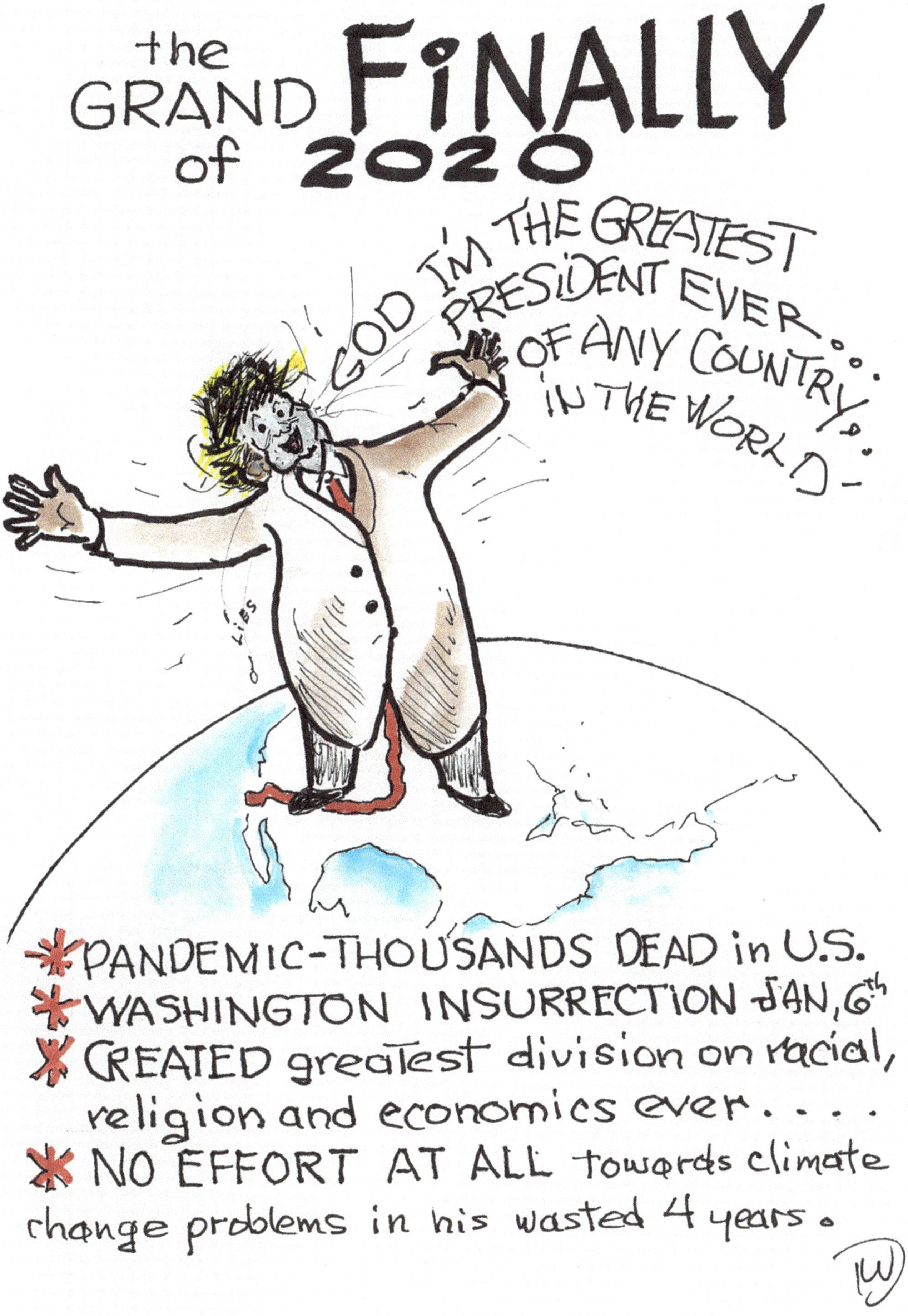
the GRAND FiNALLY of 2020
GOD I'M THE GREATEST PRESIDENT EVER... OF ANY COUNTRY... IN THE WORLD -
LIES
* PANDEMIC-THOUSANDS DEAD in U.S.
* WASHINGTON INSURRECTION JAN, 6th
* CREATED greatest division on racial, religion and economics ever....
* NO EFFORT AT ALL towards climate change problems in his wasted 4 years.
IW

Fake News

Finally! The liberation of America and the republican party from the tyranny of the democrats has been solved by our 45th president. The greatest of all our presidents has figured out, with his brillance, a catch phrase that has liberated us all from the terrible democratic war mongers. By now we all should know it. The catch phrase is "FAKE NEWS", which means every word spoken on MSNBC, 60 minutes, most newspaper, channel 4, 5, 7, T.V. etc. is democrat fake news. But, now we have Fox news! What a relief.

If you believe what is stated above, you deserve all the reprecussion of having no democracy and dealing with the whims of a dictator. This label "Fake NEWs" has already divided our country with sinister diabolical intention to change our democracy. Please believe that!

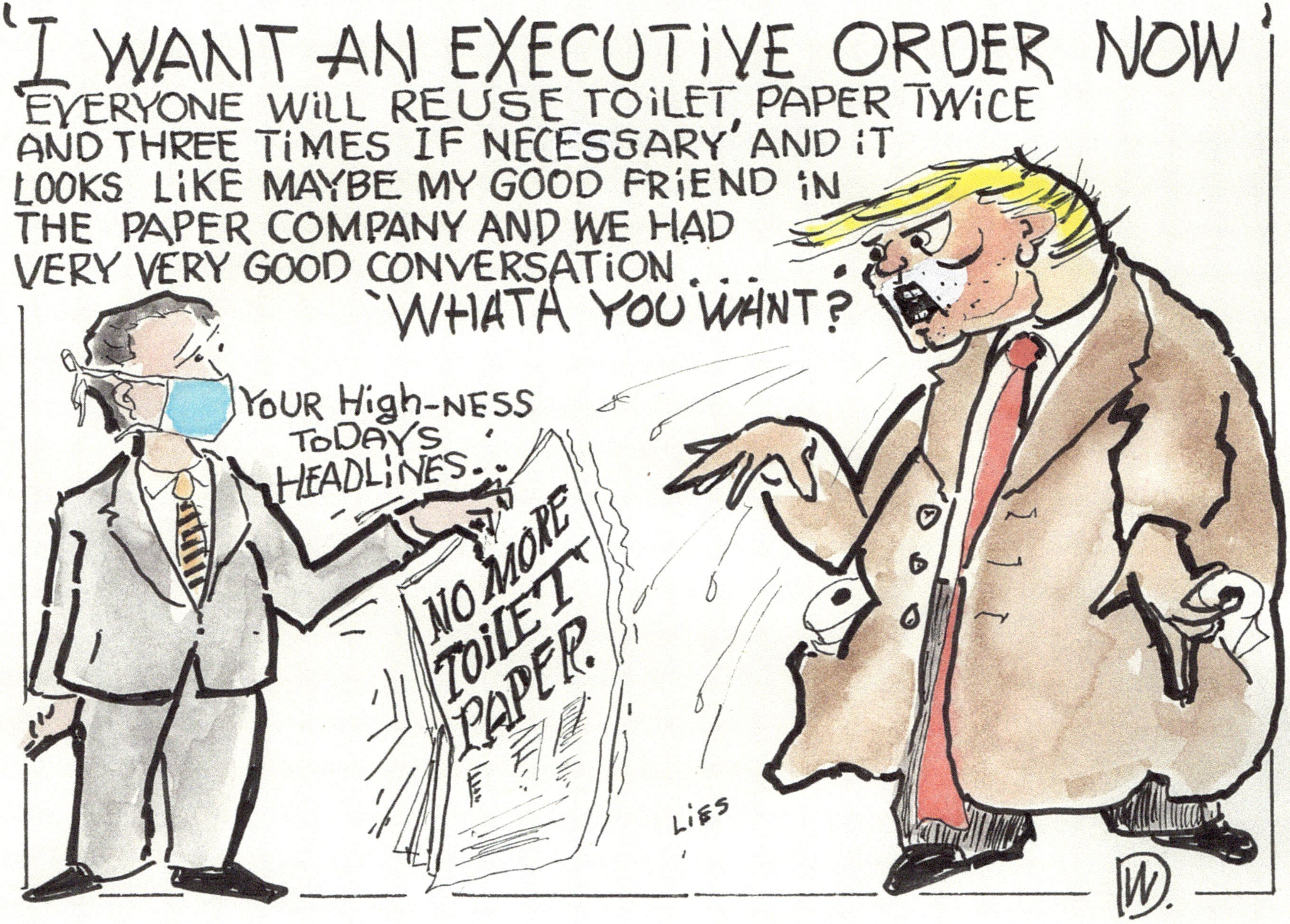
'I WANT AN EXECUTIVE ORDER NOW'
'EVERYONE WILL REUSE TOILET PAPER TWICE AND THREE TIMES IF NECESSARY' AND IT LOOKS LIKE MAYBE MY GOOD FRIEND IN THE PAPER COMPANY AND WE HAD VERY VERY GOOD CONVERSATION...
'WHATA YOU WANT?
YOUR High-NESS TODAYS HEADLINES..
NO MORE TOILET PAPER.
LIES
W.

Corruption Magnitude

Where and when did our government go astray? After the first world war? After the second world war? After the Vietnam war?

Corporate influence with its power has absorbed the realities of monopolies of the past. Corperate power has become a monsterous nemesis of wealth that has corrupted our whole political democratic system. It seems the only way to start correcting the problem would be to have a one party system which would be a democratic government composed only of a president, house of representives and supreme court. Our present republican party would no longer exist. There would be also a limit of wealth one could acquire and taxed accordingly and yes, socialized medicine would be part of the government. Insurance companies would not cover health issues. We do not need another company involved between people and health.

Present day problems can not be solved with the two party system. When the constitution was inspired in 1787 we did not have a huge corporate America, stock companies, multiple banks N.R.A. etc. putting enormous pressure to influence government to pass laws that favored their interest.

Let's make a change, now, we the people.

Is this THE END OF THE STORY?

TURN THE PAGE →

2022

Maybe a new story is about to start...

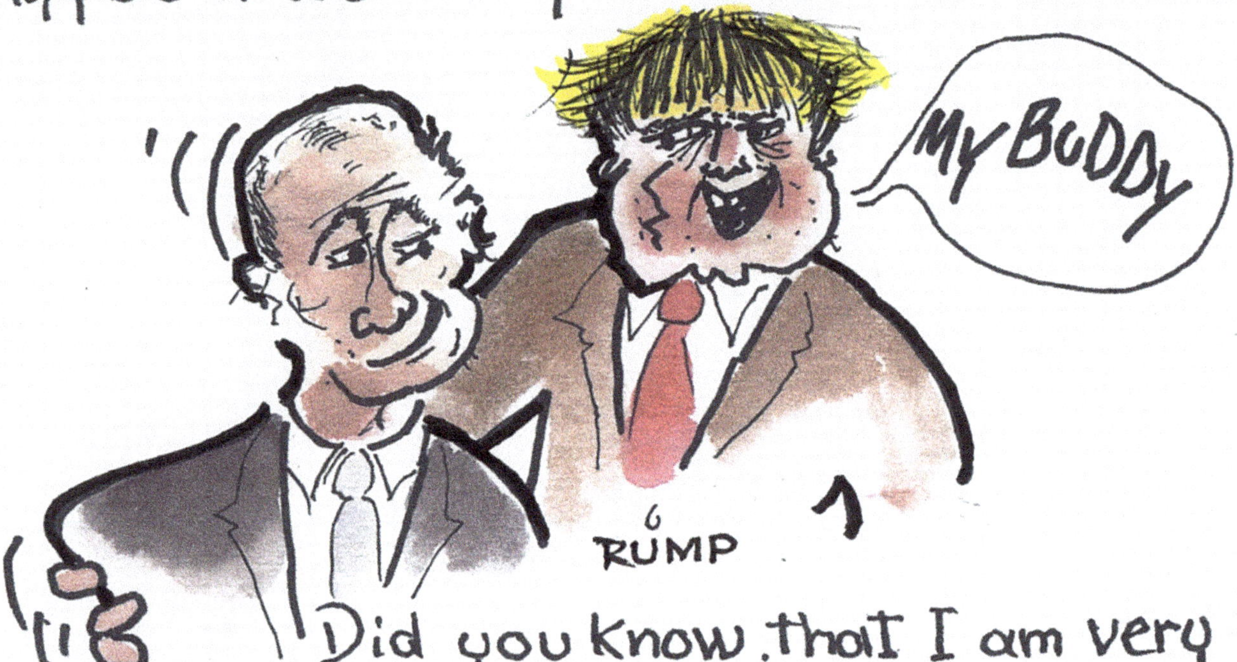
MY BUDDY
RUMP

Did you know that I am very keen in owning a nice big yacht? But first I would like to help my buddy get some more land. Because it looks like Russia has been shrinking a little bit lately.

'Vladimir', would you like Alaska, Greenland? How about Canada? You want Canada? 'You can have Canada.'

I'm going to build another wall south of the Panama Canal. 'OH BOY' Isn't this fun, 'WOW'. Me and my buddy going all over in my 1000 foot yacht.

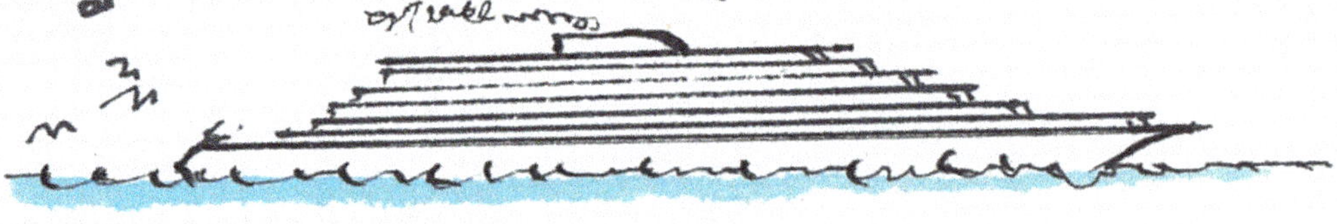

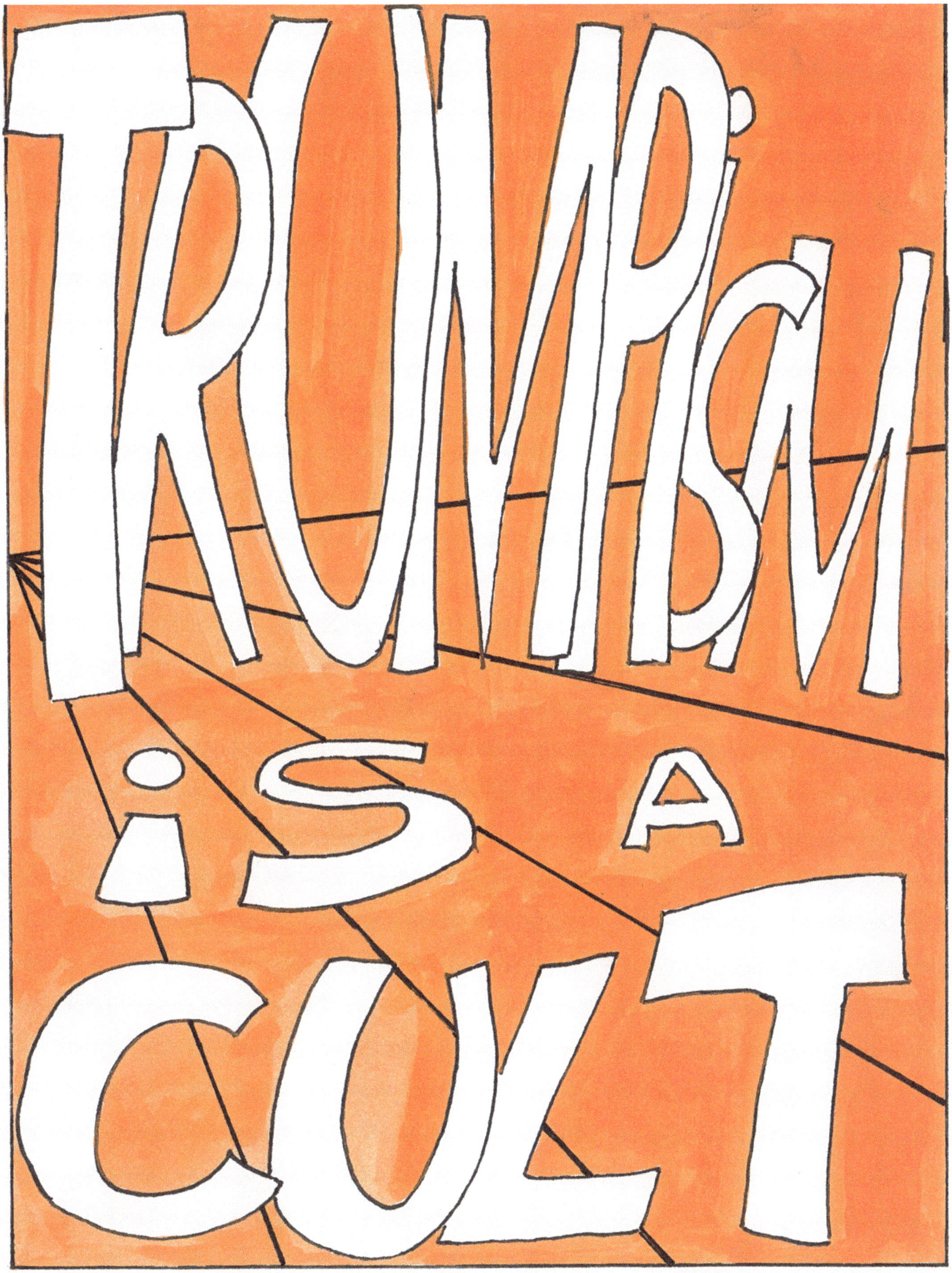
TRUMPiSM
iS A
CULT

WiTH OUT THE COOL- AiD

Certificate Of Achievement

presented to

Donald John Trump

for

Being a fat lying paranoid narcissistic schizophrenic racist misogynist thingy and is a threatening nemesis to our precious democracy.

Signed

All living things of this earth ..

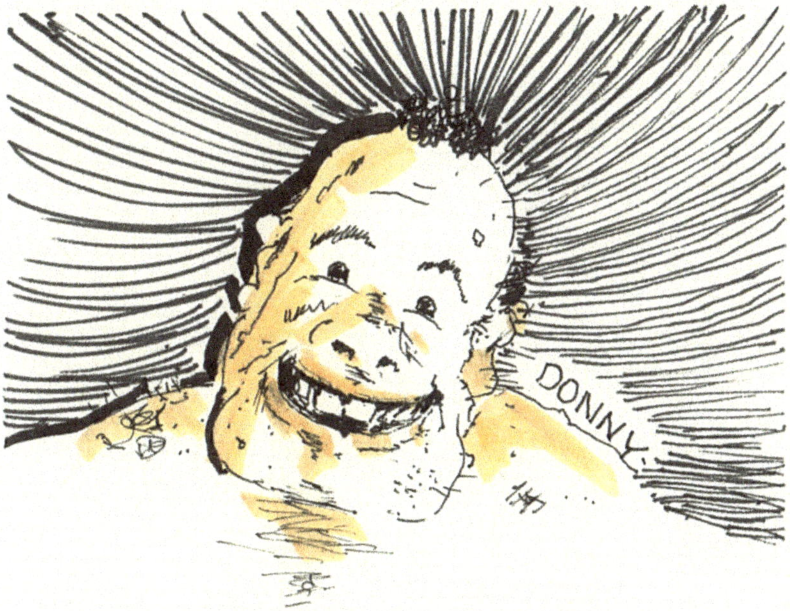
DONNY

SHOULD SUPREME
COURT JUDGES BE
POLITICALLY EMPOWERED?

www.ingramcontent.com/pod-product-compliance
Lightning Source LLC
Chambersburg PA
CBHW040007080526
44586CB00027B/2915
* 9 7 8 1 9 3 5 4 4 8 4 7 1 *